P9-EEC-770

Spiritual Growth Begins at Home

Spiritual Growth Begins at Home

LifeJourney Books is an imprint of David C. Cook
Publishing Co.
David C. Cook Publishing Co., Elgin, Illinois 60120
David C. Cook Publishing Co., Weston, Ontario
Nova Distribution, Ltd., Torquay, England

Spiritual Growth Begins at Home
©1991 by Elaine K. McEwan
(This booklet consists of selected portions of *Raising
Balanced Children in an Unbalanced World* ©1988 by
Elaine McEwan)

Edited by Brian Reck
Cover design by Bob Fuller
First printing, 1991
Printed in the United States of America
95 94 93 92 91 5 4 3 2 1

Library of Congress Cataloging in Publication Data
McEwan, Elaine K.
Spiritual Growth Begins at Home
    p. cm. — (Helping Families Grow series)
ISBN: 1-55513-656-7
1. Reading—United States—Parent participation I. Title
II. Series:
LB1050.M375   1991
649'.58—dc20   91-27568
                                           CIP

The spiritual questions of the very young child are the same ones that learned theologians ponder. Where did God come from? What is heaven like? That is probably why, when faced with such questions, we parents may stutter and stammer, leaving our children feeling much the same way they do when they ask us "Where did I come from?" Children have a sixth sense about knowing when Mom or Dad doesn't feel comfortable discussing a subject. They may never raise the question again.

We may not have a theologically eloquent answer for every question our children ask, but we must assume responsibility for their spiritual development just as we do for their intellectual, social, emotional, and physical development. The Bible tells us to "impress [these commandments] on your children. Talk about them when you sit at home and when you walk along the road, when you lie down and when you get up. Tie them as symbols on your hands and bind them on your foreheads. Write them on the doorframes of your houses and on your gates" (Deuteronomy 6:7-9).

We have no choice but to obey God's command. Just as we cannot leave the intellectual development of our children to the schools, we cannot leave their spiritual development to the church.

The spiritual dimension of a child is the most important one of all. Without it, our children will be missing out on what God has planned for their lives. This dimension includes the acceptance of Christ as personal Savior, an understanding of scriptural truths, participation in a church community, and a commitment to living out Christian values in their daily lives.

What can we as parents do to increase the likelihood that our children will develop into spiritually mature individuals? What can we do to nurture a love of God and a desire to please Him in the hearts and minds of our children? How can we ensure that our children will know the difference between right and wrong and make the right moral choices? These questions and others will be explored in the sections ahead.

WHEN DOES SPIRITUAL DEVELOPMENT BEGIN?

The spiritual development of your child begins when you bring him home from the hospital. As you rock that fretful infant in the rocking chair, begin reciting Scripture verses and telling Bible stories. Sing hymns and choruses to calm a sleepless child—and bring peace to your weary soul.

Surrounding your child with the vocabulary of worship and love will lay a foundation for his understanding of more complex concepts as he grows to maturity. The integration of worship and devotion in your home will become a natural part of your child's life.

WHAT ARE KEY AREAS OF SPIRITUAL DEVELOPMENT?

The very young child does not have the reasoning ability to comprehend complex spiritual concepts. But she can understand that God loves her in the same way her mother and father do, and that God expects her to do the right thing just as her mother and father do. An understanding of the concepts of God's love and God's authority over us will set the stage in your child's life for deeper spiritual understanding as she matures intellectually.

HOW CAN I CARE FOR MY CHILD'S SPIRITUAL WELFARE?

If you are concerned about your child's spiritual welfare then the choice of his primary caregiver (if you are away for long periods) becomes even more important. Interview this person carefully to determine how she will discipline and explain rules. A punitive and harsh caretaker may frighten your child into behaving, but will not instill the desire to do right that is your goal. Take steps to ensure that the caregiver you choose will read Bible stories aloud to your child and help instill Christian values.

WHAT SPIRITUAL PRINCIPLES CAN I TEACH MY CHILD?

Dr. James Dobson has developed a Checklist for Spiritual Training that he suggests be used as targets or goals in our spiritual nurturing of children.

Concept I: "And thou shalt love the Lord thy God with all thy heart" (Mark 12:30, KJV).

1. Is your child learning of the love of God through the love, tenderness, and mercy of his parents?
2. Is he learning to talk about the Lord, and to include Him in his thoughts and plans?
3. Is he learning to turn to Jesus when he is frightened or anxious or lonely?
4. Is he learning to read the Bible?
5. Is he learning to pray?
6. Is he learning the meaning of faith and trust?
7. Is he learning the joy of the Christian way of life?
8. Is he learning the beauty of Jesus' birth and death?

Concept II: "Thou shalt love thy neighbour as thyself" (Mark 12:31, KJV).

1. Is he learning to understand and empathize with the feelings of others?
2. Is he learning not to be selfish and demanding?
3. Is he learning to share?

4. Is he learning not to gossip and criticize others?
5. Is he learning to accept himself?

Concept III: "Teach me to do thy will; for thou art my God" (Psalm 143:10, KJV).

1. Is he learning to obey his parents as preparation for later obedience to God?
2. Is he learning to behave properly in church—God's house?
3. Is he learning a healthy appreciation for both aspects of God's nature: love and justice?
4. Is he learning that there are many forms of benevolent authority outside himself to which he must submit?
5. Is he learning the meaning of sin and its inevitable consequences?

Concept IV: "Fear God, and keep his commandments: for this is the whole duty of man" (Ecclesiastes 12:13, KJV).

1. Is he learning to be truthful and honest?
2. Is he learning to keep the Sabbath day holy?
3. Is he learning the relative

insignificance of materialism?

4. Is he learning the meaning of the Christian family, and the faithfulness to it which God intends?

5. Is he learning to follow the dictates of his own conscience?

Concept V: "But the fruit of the Spirit is . . . self-control" (Galatians 5:22, 23, RSV).

1. Is he learning to give a portion of his allowance (and other money) to God?

2. Is he learning to control his impulses?

3. Is he learning to work and carry responsibility?

4. Is he learning the vast difference between self-worth and egotistical pride?

5. Is he learning to bow in reverence before the God of the universe?

HOW CAN I ENCOURAGE MY CHILD'S SPIRITUAL DEVELOPMENT?

Parents can do many things to encourage their child's spiritual development: modeling in their own lives, taking their child to church and Sunday school, reading aloud from books that emphasize Christian values, structuring a daily devotional as part of family life, structuring a personal prayer experience for the child, teaching and training their child to develop Christian values on a consistent daily basis, answering questions and talking openly with their child about spiritual matters, and praying for their child regularly.

Our children live with us every day, and if we do not *model what we say we believe and preach*, our lessons will be meaningless. Of course, we are not perfect, but in the simple acts of family life we need to reflect the love of God. If we are preaching that God is a forgiving God, we need to model that forgiveness to our children. If we are teaching that God is a loving God, we need to model that love to our children. If we are telling our child that God wants us to love our neighbor, we need to model that love and acceptance. The Psalmist wrote:

The Lord is merciful and gracious,
Slow to anger, and plenteous in
mercy.
He will not always chide:
Neither will he keep his anger for
ever.
He hath not dealt with us after our
sins;
Nor rewarded us according to our
iniquities.
For as the heaven is high above the
earth,
So great is his mercy toward them
that fear him.
As far as the east is from the west,
So far hath he removed our
transgressions from us.
Like as a father pitieth his children,
So the Lord pitieth them that fear
him. (Psalm 103:8-13, KJV)

A more contemporary poet said this about the importance of modeling what we believe for children.

Children Live What They Learn

If a child lives with criticism,
He learns to condemn.
If a child lives with hostility,
He learns violence.
If a child lives with ridicule,
He learns to be shy.
If a child lives with shame,
He learns to feel guilty.
If a child lives with encouragement,
He learns confidence.
If a child lives with praise,
He learns to appreciate.
If a child lives with fairness,
He learns justice.
If a child lives with security,
He learns faith.
If a child lives with approval,
He learns to like himself.
If a child lives with acceptance and
 friendship,
He learns to love the world.
 —*Dorothy Law Nolte*

I think so much of that poem that I painstakingly needleworked the words in counted cross-stitch, had my finished work beautifully framed in oak, and placed it on my office wall as a testimony of what I believe about children. It hangs as a constant reminder to me, the staff, and the parents who visit that what we say is not nearly as important as what we do. Whether you work the words in counted cross-stitch, hand-letter them in calligraphy, or copy them in the front of your Bible, I suggest you keep them written in your heart.

Involvement in a *positive church environment* is another important part of nurturing a strong spiritual child. We cannot do the job alone, and a church environment where the lessons we teach at home will be explained and reinforced by trained professionals is essential to your plan for raising a child with a well-developed spiritual dimension. Attend regularly and become involved.

A wonderful way to share your faith with children is through the *read-aloud experience.* There are hundreds of wonderful children's books that retell Bible stories, show how fictional boys and girls learn the lessons of faith, and reaffirm the Christian values that parents desire in their children. I wrote *How to Raise a Reader* for that very reason. It contains age-graded selections that will help you choose the best. When your child asks a question that is difficult for you to answer in language she can understand, find a book that does it for you. If your child is having a problem with swearing or lying, find a book that tells how a fictional character is learning to obey God's commands. Sit down together and spend time reading.

Building a *family devotional time* is another important aspect of nurturing your child's spiritual dimension. Set aside time after your family dinner to worship together. In addition to reading aloud from God's Word, you can have Scripture memory contests, play Bible games, read excellent Christian literature, and pray together.

The complexity of your devotions will vary with the age of your child, but there are excellent materials to use for every age level. Researchers have long recognized the importance of the family dinner hour as the place where the culture, values, and religious beliefs of a family are shared. Do not fail to gather your family together regularly for a time of "fellowship."

Structuring a personal prayer experience for your child as soon as she is old enough to participate is another way in which you can nurture spiritual development. There are many wonderful read-aloud books that contain prayers for children. They will assist you until your child is old enough to say her own simple prayers each night before bedtime.

Christian parents need to be ready to *answer questions their children may have about spiritual matters* and be open to discussing their own relationships with God. A spiritual discussion with our children, particularly when they are older may be as difficult for us as talking about the "facts of life." Use the family devotional period to share a personal testimony. Comment on the sermon as it relates to your own personal life. Practice talking to your children about your own day-to-day walk.

The *teaching and training* of children is one of our highest callings as parents. Like us, our children are sinful creatures and must be taught the differences between right and wrong. As King Solomon said: "Foolishness is bound in the heart of a child; but the rod of correction shall drive it far from him" (Proverbs 22:15, KJV). This process is sometimes painful, but it must take place in the very early years. I watch parents struggling to teach those values to pre-adolescent children and weep with them. They have waited too long!

Our children should be at the very top of our *prayer* list. We know better than anyone in which areas of their lives they need special grace from God. If we as parents would spend as much time praying about our children as we do complaining about them to our friends, we would find their spiritual lives greatly enriched. If our children have not yet made a commitment to Christ, we should pray for their salvation. If they have made that decision, we should pray for their nurture and growth.

WHEN SHOULD I EXPECT MY CHILD TO ACCEPT CHRIST?

The years between five and ten are the most important ones in a child's life in terms of making a decision for Christ. Be sensitive to the opportunities you may have for personally leading your child to Christ. If you are unsure about just what to say or feel awkward in discussing this sensitive but all-important subject, consult one of the many excellent books that give parents guidance. (See the resources section at the end of the booklet).

WHAT SHOULD I DO WHEN MY CHILD IS DISOBEDIENT?

I am faced with this problem not only with my own children, but with the over 300 children in the elementary school where I am principal. Recently I have dealt with two sixth grade boys who stole money from the librarian's purse; two first grade boys who purposefully missed the urinal in the boys' bathroom, leaving a messy trail behind them; one fifth grade girl who skipped school for a day; and one third grade boy who swore at a teacher.

In each of these cases my approach has been the same. I told the boys and girls that what they did was wrong and why it was wrong. They broke a rule that exists in our school. I reminded them that breaking school rules has consequences and that they must make amends for their actions.

The boys who stole the money had to return what they had taken. Their parents had to come to school and have a meeting. They were given in-school suspensions. The boys who left a mess in the boys' bathroom were given a pail of soapy water and given orders to mop up their mess. The child who skipped school had to make up her time after school for several weeks. The boy who was disrespectful to the teacher received his consequences from his father, who came to school and administered a spanking in the principal's office.

Children need to have consequences for their behavior. But once they have made amends for their wrongdoing we must forget about it. No child deserves to be reminded of his sins regularly. In the case of our own children, we should remind them of God's love and forgiveness when they sin.

I tell the students in my school that I forgive them for what they have done, but am counting on them never to repeat such an incident. I tell the students I know they have made a mistake, but I tell them that I believe their problem was the result of forgetting the rules and not because they are "bad."

I make them squirm a little, because I want them to feel embarrassment and remorse for what they have done, but I also send them away feeling that the case is closed as far as I am concerned. As quickly as possible after an incident, I reestablish contact with this youngster to affirm my positive feelings for him.

THE DEVASTATING DOZEN

I recently held two-week-old Sarah in my arms. Although she weighed over eight pounds at birth, she seemed fragile and almost breakable. Her sweet rosebud mouth and dove-soft skin gave her an even more vulnerable quality. She will be totally dependent on her parents for all of her needs for quite some time.

The poignant memories of my experiences as a brand-new mother flooded through my mind as I held this baby. Would I want to begin again? Absolutely not. Are there some things I'd do differently? Probably! Do I have major regrets about anything I've done? Definitely not!

Our goal as parents is to launch our children into the world knowing that, although we've made mistakes along the way and there are some things we wish we'd done differently, overall we feel good about our experiences as parents, and we like and respect our children.

Although children are hearty souls who can usually survive our minor shortcomings as parents, there are several major child-rearing patterns that will seriously inhibit the development of a well-rounded child. The strong presence of any one of these family patterns will impact a child's development to varying degrees, but put them together and the results can be absolutely devastating.

Here are some potentially harmful child-rearing practices:

- Live your life through your child.
- Try to put a square peg in a round hole.
- Make all of your child's decisions.
- Give your child everything he wants, including his own way.
- Be punitive, unloving, and unrealistic toward your child.
- Deprive your child of the normal growing up experiences.
- Expect your child to be a psychological "wunderkid."
- Force your child to grow up too fast.

The major problem with the above list is that each of these practices exists on a continuum. As parents, we choose at what point on that continuum we will position ourselves—what choices we will make as we raise our children.

Each of these practices in and of itself has good in it. After all, don't we need to make some decisions for our children? At times they don't have enough judgment or wisdom to make their own. Don't we need to have family expectations and standards for our children? They won't do anything if we don't express our expectations for them. Shouldn't we share our family's resources with our children? We certainly don't want them to be deprived. Don't we need rules and consequences in our families? Children would run wild without them. The biblical admonition of "moderation in all things" should stand as a constant reminder to us as we choose where on the continuum we wish to fall as we raise our children.

DON'T LIVE YOUR LIFE THROUGH YOUR CHILD

We lived near a family for several years that was trying to do this very thing. They seemed to have a dozen boys judging from the noise that emanated from their open windows during summer nights. Actually, there were only six. "Boys will be boys" was their parents' motto, and that phrase seemed to cover a multitude of neighborhood sins.

Their father was very proud of them. He spoke of his unfulfilled dream to play college football, but he said with assurance,

"My boys are going to get athletic scholarships to college. They're going to be football players."

Each fall, boys of varying sizes would walk past my window, outfitted for football practice at the nearby park. But the oldest son of that neighbor family caught my eye. He seemed dwarfed by the size of his helmet. A scrawny kid, his shoulders drooped with the weight of the shoulder pads. He dragged his feet slowly down the sidewalk, as if to postpone the eventuality of a strenuous practice. His body language said "I hate to play football."

The family moved away before the boy reached high school, but my guess is that if he played sports at all, he took up golf or tennis—a sport more suited to his physical size and build. The same scene is replayed hundreds of times in our society, as parents who weren't successful in their own attempts at a career or sport force their children to play out those dreams.

DON'T TRY TO PUT A SQUARE PEG IN A ROUND HOLE

Putting a square peg in a round hole is somewhat similar to the previous pattern of living your life through your child, but there is one subtle difference. In this child-rearing practice, highly successful and competent parents attempt to duplicate their own lives in their children. Doctors try to raise young doctors; musicians want their children to join the family musical group; successful businessmen want junior to take over the family business.

But what if junior is an artist in a family that has always played football? What if the eldest daughter wants to become a lawyer, while her mother thinks she should marry and settle down? What if your child wants to be a Presbyterian and you've always been Baptist?

I sometimes look at my own two children and wonder how they could be so different, not only from each other, but also from their parents. They are both highly successful in their own endeavors and respect each other's achievements, but they are different. My husband and I have nurtured and encouraged those differences, permitting each child to be an individual.

DON'T MAKE ALL OF YOUR CHILD'S DECISIONS

Several years ago, I enrolled a new fifth-grade student in our school. He came to us from a private school, where his lack of academic success was causing his parents' grave concerns. The school was frustrated about their inability to meet his needs and suggested to the parents that the public school might be able to help him. He was a handsome boy, well-dressed, and extremely polite. I was optimistic about our chances for giving this child success.

Several weeks later, I had begun to observe a pattern. Jason's mother was at school nearly every day. If she didn't come to school, she called. The secretary was always leaving messages in his teacher's box. Although their house was well within walking distance, she picked him up every day in the car. Not trusting Jason to come to the car alone, she sent an older sister up to his classroom to fetch him. Not believing that Jason could take the responsibility for his homework assignments, she continually asked the teacher to write out a special assignment list.

I questioned the teacher about Jason's progress, and she answered, "Jason would be fine if his mother would leave him alone. He's a great kid, but she's smothering him."

Sometimes we have to let our children make their own decisions, make their own mistakes, and take responsibility for what happens to them. This process begins when children are very small, for if we don't permit them to make some choices about what to eat, what to wear, and how to spend their time as very small children, we will create dependent and emotionally crippled persons.

DON'T GIVE YOUR CHILD EVERYTHING HE WANTS

In a society that is oriented to material wealth, our children quickly learn to "want things." And parents come to realize that their own guilt feelings about child rearing can be assuaged by "buying their kids off." Working parents are particularly vulnerable to this unfortunate child-rearing pattern. After all, I rationalize to myself, I'm working to provide extras for my family because I love them. And when I'm unable to spend time with them, I fall prey to giving them more than they should have.

Our children will quickly become cynical and learn how to manipulate our vulnerability to get exactly what they want. And don't think that teenagers are the only group that learn this skill. Haven't you watched a clever four year old talk his mother into a toy or a candy bar at the supermarket checkout because she feels guilty about something? We must learn to say no to our children's insatiable appetites, and we must also guard against buying them off to compensate for something we haven't done.

Our high school parking lot is filled with shiny late model cars—Saabs and BMWs. These cars do not belong to the teachers; they belong to the students. I suspect that many of them represent "payoffs" to kids.

I work very hard at not falling into the trap of giving my children everything they want, but for me personally, this area of parenting is the most difficult. I hate to say no to my children when they ask for something, particularly if I have the resources to pay for it. But experience and common sense tell me I'm making a big mistake when I do.

Each family must evaluate where they will draw the line with regard to indulging their children's material wants. Children are masters at "conspicuous consumption," and we must take care we do not fall into the trap of creating "materialistic monsters."

Material possessions are not the only area in which parents give children whatever they want. We do the same thing when we let them have their own way, when we never discipline or correct our children. The most challenging child for a teacher to deal with is one whose parent has never said "no." The most frustrating situation for a principal to deal with is a parent who thinks his child has never done anything wrong.

I can almost predict, when I hand out a discipline notice to a certain group of children, that the telephone will be ringing about 3:15. Johnny's mother is on the phone to tell me that Johnny didn't do it. I can hear Johnny whining in the background as he protests his innocence to his mother. In those cases, Johnny, his mother, the principal, and the person who caught Johnny in the act will gather in the principal's office. Johnny's mother is usually shocked and dismayed to find out that Johnny has lied. She is embarrassed, annoyed, and can't understand how this could have happened. The answer is simple. She never said "no" to Johnny.

DON'T BE PUNITIVE, UNLOVING OR UNREALISTIC TO YOUR CHILD

Dr. Paul Meier has developed a checklist of child-rearing practices that create emotionally disturbed children. He says that if you want to develop an obsessive child you "expect perfect etiquette and manners from your child from his day of birth on. Don't tolerate any mistakes." It also helps to "be very critical of the people around you—this includes your minister, your neighbors, your husband, and, most importantly, your child."

"If you really want to do the job right," he says, "emphasize the letter of the law rather than the spirit of the law. Make your rules quite rigid, and never allow any exceptions." Of course you'll also want to "practice the Victorian ethic. Shame your child for being a sexual being." Obsessive children are "excessively rigid, over-inhibited, over-conscientious, over-dutiful, and unable to relax easily." In our zeal to raise children who obey God's Word, we must be especially careful not to fall into the terrible trap of expecting perfection.

DON'T DEPRIVE YOUR CHILD OF NORMAL EXPERIENCES

I attended Wheaton College for my under-graduate degree and had the privilege of getting to know many "missionary kids." These young people had frequently attended boarding schools from their earliest years, seeing their parents only once or twice a year. They were often deprived of the "normal experiences" of growing up with family. In many cases they were bitter and rebellious about Christianity. In other cases, they were withdrawn, insecure, and socially inept.

Another practice that has the potential for depriving children of normal growing up experiences is home schooling. This represents my rather biased view as a public school principal—we think we can do it better. What we do better is not necessarily "teach" the basics, however. That job can be accomplished quite nicely at home by an effective parent. With appropriate textbooks, adequate time, and good teaching, kids can learn the subject matter of school anywhere.

What we do provide in school are the normal experiences of "growing up." How do you get along with a large group? How do you share the attention of an adult with others? How do you cope with the idea that someone else is smarter, faster, richer, or prettier than you? How do you live the Christian life with temptations around you? Where do you practice the Christian values and virtues that you learn in Sunday school? You only learn these lessons in group settings away from your parents.

DON'T EXPECT YOUR CHILD TO BE A "WUNDERKID"

I recently heard a management consultant discussing his own personal child-rearing practices. As parents of a five year old, he and his wife, a practicing psychologist, were committed to their careers. He shared that they have discussions with their child about the place of work in their lives and have told him that their work is the most important thing to both of them.

He assured his listeners that children need to know where they stand with regard to their parents' priorities. They'll relate far better to this type of approach, he concluded, than to a father and mother who say their children are first and then spend all of their time working. They can't cope, he added, with hypocrisy.

I listened in amazement to this psychological nonsense. What made him think that a child of five could relate to the jargon and "priorities" of a modern career couple? Was he relieving his own guilt by engaging in this "encounter group process" with a child? We must be careful lest we give our children too much credit for their understanding of "modern psychology." We must also realize that glib phrases and facile discussion of such heady concepts as careers and priorities fall on deaf ears if those ears belong to a young child.

Single parents often fall into this same trap. In their loneliness and frustration, they turn to their children to act as counselors. They share financial concerns and problems with dating and open up to their children in ways that are damaging to the parent-child relationship. Children are not psychologically or emotionally ready to play the role of counselor or advisor to their parents. Children lose important chunks of their childhood when they are forced to pretend a psychological maturity beyond their years.

DON'T FORCE YOUR CHILD TO GROW UP TOO FAST

Children are forced to grow up too fast if they are asked to wear clothing, engage in activities, and learn skills that are beyond them emotionally, physically, and psychologically. Parents who dress their toddlers in designer clothes, enroll them in ice skating and swimming lessons at three and four, send them to academic prep schools in infancy, and expect Olympic medals in adolescence are forcing their children to grow up too fast.

Television commercials perpetrate this particularly offensive practice. Little girls barely out of diapers dress, speak, and act like adults, making those of us with normal children wonder why our kids don't look like Hollywood models.

Childhood is developmental. Kids need time to develop. Working parents who expect children to cook meals, clean the house, and assume adult responsibilities are forcing their children to grow up too fast. Again, good judgment must prevail. Children need chores. Children need responsibilities. Children need to grow up. But they don't need to do it at fast forward. They need to spend as much time in child-hood games as possible. They will be better adjusted adults as a result.

Although a new baby is fragile and vulnerable, she is also amazingly resilient and flexible. In the years ahead, as she grows, her parents will make many mis-takes. We all do. But her parents hope the mistakes will be minor ones. They will monitor and self-correct. As husband and wife, they will talk about their child's spiritual, psychological, emotional, physical, and intellectual development. They will seek out the advice of professionals if they see problems arising. But most importantly, they will be seeking God's counsel for the most critical task they can undertake as husband and wife—raising a balanced child!

WHERE CAN I GO FOR MORE INFORMATION?

If you are interested in reading more about healthy family life, many excellent books will give you other perspectives. Books with a Christian emphasis are designated with an asterisk.

*How to Talk With Your Children About God** (Frances Loftiss Carroll, Prentice-Hall, Inc., 1985)—Step-by-step helps for parents in just what to say and how to say it. If you find it difficult to talk about spiritual concepts with children, this book will give you courage.

*Building Your Child's Faith** (Alice Chapin, Here's Life Publishers, 1983)—This outstanding little paperback has a helpful chapter on when to teach what as well as ten-minute-a-day Bible readings for children. This book is a must for every parent who wishes to bring up a spiritual child.

How to Make Your Child a Winner (Victor B. Cline, Walker and Company, 1980)—Chapters 6 (Conscience and Moral Values: Keep Your Kid Out of Jail) and 7 (How to Teach Your Child to Be Responsible) are good resources.

*Dr. Dobson Answers Your Questions** (James Dobson, Tyndale House Publishers, 1982)— A section on spiritual training is contained in this helpful compilation of questions parents commonly ask.

*Building Your Child's Character From the Inside Out** (Kay Kuzma, David C. Cook, 1988)—Significant help in nurturing and molding your child's character, using the "in" steps of instruction, influence and inner control.

*Rights, Wrongs, and In-Betweens** (Jim Larson, Augsburg House, 1984)—Contains guidelines for using the Bible to identify values, a sketch of moral development, and family activities to do together.

*Keeping Your Teen in Touch with God** (Robert Laurent, David C. Cook, 1988)—Superb insights based on extensive research and experience. Contains a special emphasis on the relationship of the church and the home.

Raising Good Children (Thomas Lickona, Bantam Books, 1983)—This book contains many practical ideas for instilling such basic values as honesty, courtesy, and respect.

How to Motivate Your Child Toward Success*
(William Steuart McBirnie, Tyndale House,
1979)—Chapters 7 (The Christian Education
of Your Child) and 8 (How to Lead Your
Child to Christ) will give you additional
help as you seek to nurture spiritual values
in your child's life.

How to Raise a Reader* (Elaine K. McEwan,
David C. Cook, 1987)—If you're wondering
what to read aloud to encourage spiritual
growth in your child, this volume will help
you. Bible story books, scriptural application
books, and fiction that emphasizes Christian
values are included for all age levels.

*Christian Child-Rearing and Personality
Development** (Paul D. Meier, Baker Book
House, 1977)—Meier discusses spiritual
development within the context of personality development. Meier's discussion about
how to choose the appropriate church environment for your children is especially good.

Bringing Up a Moral Child (Michael Schulman
and Eva Mekler, Addison-Wesley Publishing
Co., Inc., 1985)—A very complete volume
that examines moral development through
the various stages of childhood.

*The Christian Family** (Larry Christenson, Bethany House Publishers, 1970)—Christenson writes eloquently on the power of the Christian family. This book has stood the test of time.

Traits of a Healthy Family (Dolores Curran, Ballantine Books, 1983)—This paperback volume sets forth fifteen traits that characterize a healthy family. See if yours measures up.

*Parents Take Charge** (Perry L. Draper, Tyndale House,1982)—Thirteen lessons for use in small group discussions to help parents learn the spiritual and psychological lessons that are needed to raise children.

*Seven Things Children Need** (John M. Drescher, Herald Press, 1976)—According to Drescher, children need significance, security, acceptance, love, praise, discipline, and God.

*Christian Child-Rearing and Personality Development** (Paul Meier, Baker Book House, 1977)—Especially interesting is the chapter entitled "How to Develop Emotionally Disturbed Children." It includes sections on how to raise a drug addict, alcoholic, homosexual, sociopathic criminal, hysterical daughter, adult schizophrenic, obsessive, accident prone, obese or anorexic child, enuretic or encopretic child, and a hyperactive child.

*How to Keep Your Kids On Your Team**
(Charles Stanley, Oliver Nelson, 1986)—
Charles Stanley is among my favorites in his approach to healthy family life. He is proactive rather than reactive and his principles are a good blend of common sense and biblical wisdom.

*Raising Positive Kids in a Negative World**
(Zig Ziglar, Oliver Nelson, 1985)—Although the emphasis is on "pop psychology" and "positive thinking," you will find some interesting and motivating ideas.

HELPING FAMILIES GROW SERIES

❧ *Communicating Spiritual Values Through Christian Music*

❧ *Equipping Your Child for Spiritual Warfare*

❧ *Family Vacations that Work*

❧ *Helping Your Child Stand Up to Peer Pressure*

❧ *How to Discover Your Child's Unique Gifts*

❧ *How to Work With Your Child's Teachers*

❧ *Helping Your Child Love to Read*

❧ *Improving Your Child's Self-Image*

❧ *Preparing for Your New Baby*

❧ *Should My Child Listen to Rock Music?*

❧ *Spiritual Growth Begins At Home*

❧ *Surviving the Terrible Teenage Years*

ABOUT THE AUTHOR

Dr. Elaine McEwan is the author of *How to Raise a Reader*, *Will My Child Be Ready for School?* and *Raising Balanced Children in a Balanced World*.

Her experience in raising balanced children was partially acquired while bringing up her own children, Emily and Patrick, and has been supplemented through her experience as elementary school teacher, librarian, and school principal (her current job)

Elaine is a graduate of Wheaton College and holds a doctorate in education from Northern Illinois University. She lives in Wheaton, Illinois.